I AM

REFLECTIONS FOR PARENTS
OF CHILDREN WITH EATING DISORDERS

RECOVERING

A mother's journey
and her own recovery

TOO

Galia Carolina Smith MSc, PhD.

*"To be a parent for your child
is also to be a parent for yourself".*

Miguel de Cervantes

INTRODUCTION

In August 2014, English doctors diagnosed my daughter with an eating disorder, anorexia. At the time, I could not grasp the depth of this discovery, nor the impact it would have on her. I was simply unaware of the complex reality that awaited us. I took her out of school, thinking she would be with me for at most two months, convinced that her health merited it. We spent three years together at home. My daughter managed to finish her secondary education, meeting all the necessary requirements despite the interminable onslaught of challenges we faced as a result of her condition. Even though she returned to an academic institution to continue with her secondary diploma, the disorder continued to lurk about her daily life, like a silent threat.

She crossed through many dark passages, and I was there watching it all. What began as anxiety-induced overeating at age eleven, passed through a bulimic phase, and ended in purgative anorexia.

The first years of my personal experience were heartbreaking because of my lack of knowledge and specialised medical guidance. It's been seven years since then, and the battle continues, albeit from another place. A place where she can handle the situation herself with professional support. A place of natural and legitimate aspirations for a functional life. A place of personal enquiry into her strengths and limitations and the unconditional love that my husband and I give her at home.

I have kept a log of my learning throughout this journey, in the hope that it will find its way into the hands of a parent or loved one interested in hearing about a real life experience of someone who has dealt with an eating disorder. I am aware that every experience is unique, individual and dynamic. Mine is no exception. This compendium therefore only captures what I went through as a mother, and how I learned from it. This story is a tribute to the warrior spirit of every son or daughter suffering with anorexia, or bulimia or both, and underscores the vital roles of both mother and father. I invite you to discover how I sought to love my daughter. It's neither good nor bad. I am not a good or bad mother, I am simply a mother. When I couldn't find the words to make sense of it all, I drew. The images explained what I couldn't understand through words. It was just like that. This is my story.

"For you, a thousand times over".

Khaled Hosseini

ACKNOWLEDGMENTS

Few people witnessed this seven-year journey from start to finish. More than anything else, discretion prevailed when it came to sharing my daughter's suffering. She has her truth, her journey and a living experience of an eating disorder. I owe a debt of gratitude for everything that I can express in this book first and foremost to her. She taught and continues to teach me the wonder and irrefutable experience of being alongside her on her journey. In these pages, I briefly share my open truth on what I've gone through, what I've felt, and my quest to learn how to be the mother she needed.

May 2022

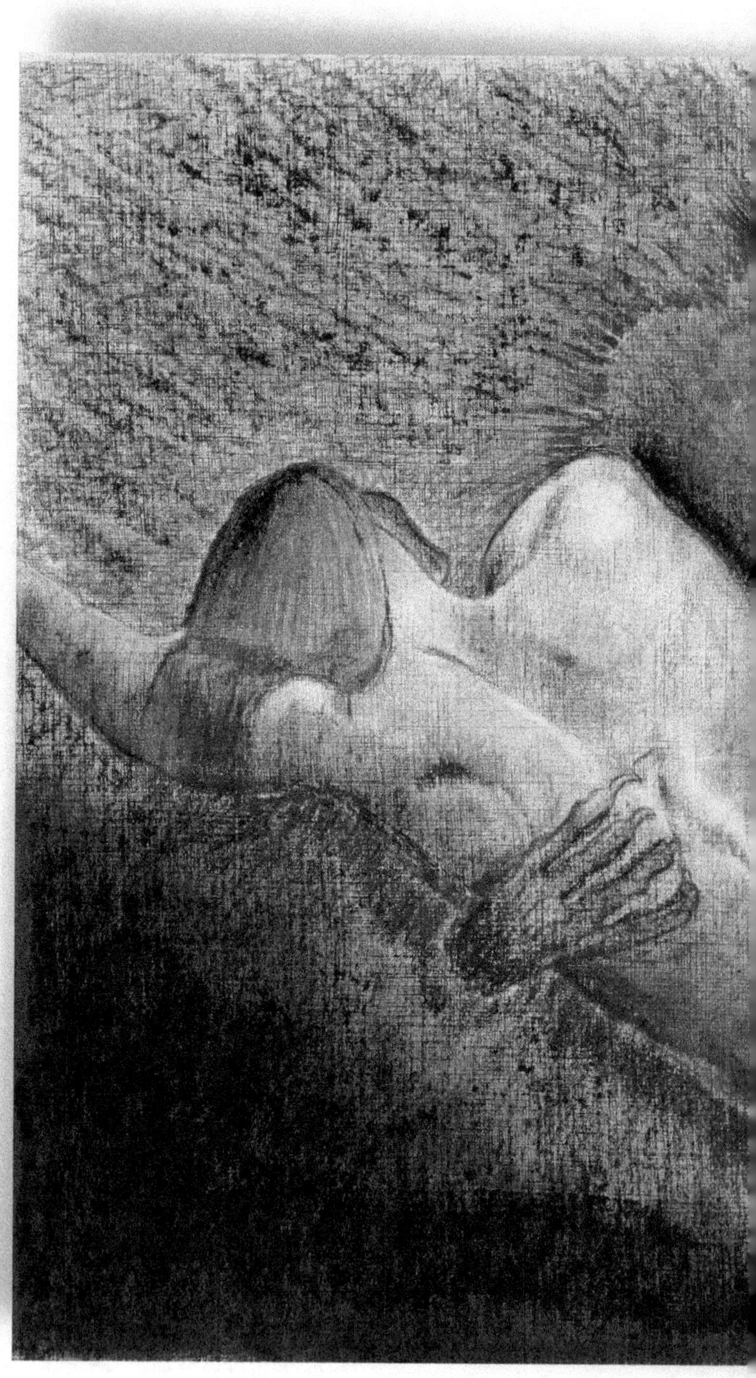

I AM RECOVERING TOO

DAY 1

My twelve-year-old daughter has lost a lot of weight. She had always enjoyed eating. Now I think she looks too thin. This prompted me to call the general practitioner, who told me to take her to his office for a check-up. While I am no medical specialist, listening to my daughter's answers in the consulting room was rather alarming. The doctor suggested an immediate referral to the children's clinic specialising in eating disorders.

Her weakened heart from a weight loss of over fifteen kilos in less than six months reminds me how fragile life is. Paralysed, I look at her and I still can't understand what happened. The session with the child psychiatrist was devastating. Carefully choosing her words, the psychiatrist revealed that my daughter's problem would take at least ten years of multidisciplinary treatment for a possible recovery, though we had to understand that there are no certainties. She concluded by warning us that we were looking at a life-threatening psychiatric illness.

Seeing a child suffering from a life-threatening illness can weaken our bodies and even prevent us from acting and responding. After receiving the diagnosis, I felt very strange back at home; an autopilot sensor went off in me. It was the autopilot of doing. I sought to care for my daughter in a suffocating and exasperated manner. Days kept passing and I couldn't stop moving. I couldn't sleep either. Suddenly, after two or three weeks, I felt a sharp physical pain around my heart, forcing me to take a break. The pain was so strong, I could only cry. I wept for several hours in helplessness at the news of my daughter's condition. I was terrified of losing her.

"Some of the greatest heroes have confessed that just before they fell to [began combat] they had a sinking [feeling in the stomach]".

Peter Pan (James Matthew Barrie)

DAY 2

The local public health service recommended that we attend parent support groups. My husband and I go, but it proves difficult for me. They encourage us to participate, yet I am at a loss for words. I struggle to even structure the words to describe the thick cloud that had settled in my mind. Listening to each and every parent pour out so much pain is nauseating. Their stories, full of suffering, soaked in helplessness, sends shivers down my spine. I stop listening and just tune them out. While I am used to feeling the pain of others through my work as a sociologist studying vulnerable populations, my brain failed to respond this time. I just feel like I'm going to fall off my chair.

My husband and I decided that he would attend the parent support group, while I stay at home with our daughter. He took a few days off work and began reading the published material they gave us. I thought I needed time to digest and allow this new reality to settle inside me. I anxiously seek mental calm amidst this storm.

"It is our choices, Harry, that show what we truly are, far more than our abilities".

Harry Potter and the Chamber of Secrets (J.K. Rowling)

DAY 3

I want to understand what an eating disorder is. I read published material again and again. Everything in it says that it is a serious mental health condition. A persistent pattern of unhealthy eating associated with a way of thinking about food. As a result, you can eat much less or much more than your body needs. This behaviour is associated with emotional, physical, social or any other type of distress. While I understand the theoretical aspect of eating disorders, I can't connect it with the traumatic and terrifying experience that my daughter is going through.

My somewhat obsessive drive to understand what is happening to my daughter spurs me to research into the literature, looking at the experiences of adults who have dealt with this same illness. I conclude that my twelve-year-old daughter is the victim of a thought-invading guest that arbitrarily foisted a way of relating to food on her. This guest has gradually become a dictator, pushing my daughter's true personality into a corner. This guest, in this case anorexia, has a voice and feeds on the human body. Every time my daughter loses weight it is because the anorexia has become stronger and the voice it speaks with becomes more powerful. I see my daughter terrified if she does not obey the tyrant. Last night I dreamt that anorexia was a monkey, more like an aggressive baboon. A manipulative entity. Although it sounds a bit dramatic and laden with imaginary weight, such a visualisation has helped me to understand it. I decided to draw it.

"There is something more important than logic: imagination".

Alfred Hitchcock

DAY 4

I have started reading the parenting materials and I notice that our daughter is showing symptoms of the disease. I had assumed these behaviours to be part of her personality, but now that I think about it, they may not be traits that describe her, but something that requires attention; for example, her being so quiet for hours at a time (behaviour that was unusual for her), or a somewhat inordinate willingness to please everyone. I often see her as terrified, vulnerable and emotionally fragile. She attempts to avoid all social contact. I see her undergoing a kind of regression, as if she wanted company without admitting it. She has ordered baby purees and wants me to buy her foods that come in very small cubes. She lies in a foetal position on her bed as I offer her the company she craves.

Not all children will behave in the same way as described in the books. However, in reading about how the disease manifests itself, I discover how difficult it is to discern between changes in behaviour as a result of the normal evolution of children at that age and those that are caused exclusively by the disease. Only a loving and genuine approach from a parent can help to clarify what is going on with her and what she needs.

"Things aren't always what they seem".

Aladdin (John August, Guy Ritchie and Vanessa Taylor)

I AM RECOVERING TOO

© Galia Carolina Smith MSc, PhD.

DAY 5

I fall into despair when I see my daughter in distress, and I think that somehow I must help her to solve her problem. That, I believe, is the job of every parent. I know that eating disorders take a long time to develop and their treatment requires knowledge, understanding and patience. That is why, as the days go by, I often ask myself: What is my role as a mother of a twelve-year-old girl with an eating disorder? Deep down, I know my task is to accompany her, which, may seem little, but is really a lot. Simply being there for her: my presence, my listening, my concern, my best wish for her to get better; that's the task. Additionally, the best thing I can do is to follow the guidelines set by the healthcare professionals specialising in eating disorders who see my daughter. I must resist the desire to control everything and everyone around me.

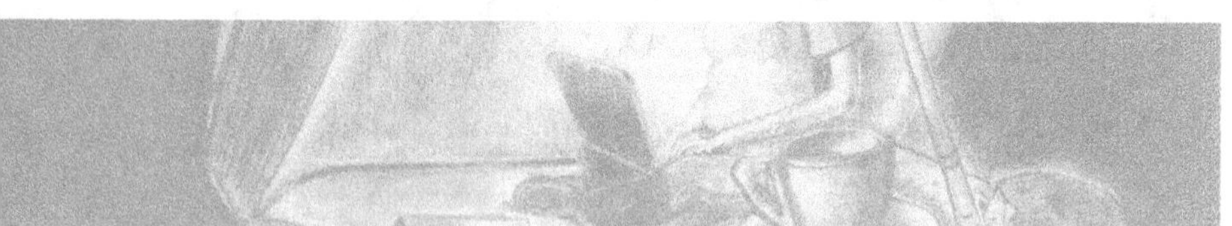

There is a fine line between controlling behaviour (by someone who usually feels insecure) and caring behaviour (from someone who selflessly looks out for the other person's health and wellbeing). They come from different places, but can be very similar. Being controlling distances people, being caring brings them together. When my daughter doesn't want to follow the food and behavioural guidelines, I get angry. Did that anger come because she didn't follow the guidelines? Or because she didn't do what I said? There are a thousand and one ways to understand the guidelines, to walk through them with her so that she is better and finds them manageable. There is only one way to please a controlling mother, and that is to blindly obey the lady's ego.

"What she needed was just one person, one wise and sympathetic grown-up, who could help her to understand".

Matilda (Roald Dahl)

DAY 6

It amazes me how my daughter has the number of calories in her head for everything she eats! My goodness, she's a walking calculator! Her mathematical ability is astonishing. Unfortunately, she is using it to give free rein to her illness. She is a very smart girl with a very high potential to go far in whatever she sets her mind to. On the other hand, I see that she refuses to eat anything she can't quantify in calories. Eating disorders definitely have one common rationale: wanting control.

Actually seeing this control component as an essential part of an eating disorder in action also challenges my own desire to control. I realise that it is possible to get the whole family hooked on one game of trying to control the other. My daughter will want to control what she eats and I will want to control what she doesn't eat. It may be important to give her spaces of control where she can exercise autonomy, such as when she chooses her clothes, personal style, the way she does her hair, or where she goes with her friends. And to shut down any possibility of her being able to choose her dinner or the size of her portions. These will continue to be served as indicated in the menu provided to us.

"One must demand of each and every one what he or she is capable of".

The Little Prince (Antoine de Saint-Exupéry)

DAY 7

I am overwhelmed by the thought that I am to blame for my daughter's eating disorder. At times I pretend that the eating disorders are not so serious and that my daughter is going to be fine. Other times I get angry and often cry inconsolably. It's okay to feel this, just let it out. However, there is no point in looking for culprits. The disorder arises from a combination of factors. I deliberately choose to live in the present; she is here today and I am here today. I feel grateful.

"I don't have an eating disorder". That was an interesting observation I made to the therapist on duty once, when he suggested that I seek psychotherapy. I didn't see the need. Perhaps because I felt that by choosing to be treated psychologically I was admitting that, in some way, my daughter's eating disorder was my fault. I look at things differently today. Whether it was my fault or not is irrelevant. Why is my ego dancing here? Regardless of whether I have disordered eating or an eating disorder, it is essential to understand it and psychological therapy will help me to cope with it better. Besides, how can I help my daughter's recovery if I don't even understand what recovery means? My own recovery should begin with an understanding of what recovery entails. Moreover, if helping myself means that I can help my daughter and support her better, then I welcome the therapy; I want to give it a chance.

"You can't stay in your corner of the forest waiting for others to come to you. You have to go to them sometimes".

Winnie-the-Pooh (Alan Alexander Milne)

DAY 8

When I first sensed that something was not right with my daughter, I debated in my mind whether she really did have an eating disorder. Although she had lost a lot of weight, it was probably only temporary, no cause for alarm. However, something inside me insisted that things were not good at all. Her cheerful and jovial temperament seemed to have been extinguished. I talked to other mothers and sought affirmation from them. I started reading about childhood and changes in children, and was reassured to learn that the experts weren't all that clear. However, I had begun to lose my inner peace.

There is a personal truth that lives inside every mother. True courage leads us to stop avoiding that motherly voice and to listen to it. That constant light calls us to act when our children need it. Today, I let my mother's voice guide me to know how to help my daughter; to strengthen me in difficult moments and in calm ones. Even when I have exhausted all my resources, this little voice tells me that the best thing to do is to let go and let my daughter find herself, let health professionals guide her, and me too.

"It is only with the heart that one can see rightly; What is essential is invisible to the eye".

The Little Prince (Antoine de Saint-Exupéry)

DAY 9

The few times my daughter consents to engage in relatively in-depth and sustained conversations with me, she seems to go off the deep end. It kind of makes no sense what she says. She tells me that she is scared of food, which sounds very strange. At other times she tells me that I don't love her, that I find her unpleasant and ugly. It saddens me that she thinks that. And there are other times when she asks me to help her, when she admits that she doesn't know why she feels so bad, that inside her head someone is swearing at her and she doesn't like to listen to it. She feels guilty and mortified about what is happening to her.

The reading material clearly points out that one is the voice of the girl or boy with the disorder and another the voice of the illness. The disease usually manifests itself through behaviours or words that point to the very thing that is harmful to the patient. From the disease comes a fear of fat, carbohydrates, dairy foods, or any food that can help regain lost body weight. From the disease itself comes the fear of all that my daughter could enjoy. All negative, destructive or health-threatening content also comes from the disease. My task has been to discern which is the voice of my daughter and which is the voice of the disease.

"If one knew, he wondered, the facts, would one have to feel pity even for the planets? if one reached what they called the heart of the matter?".

Graham Greene

I AM RECOVERING TOO

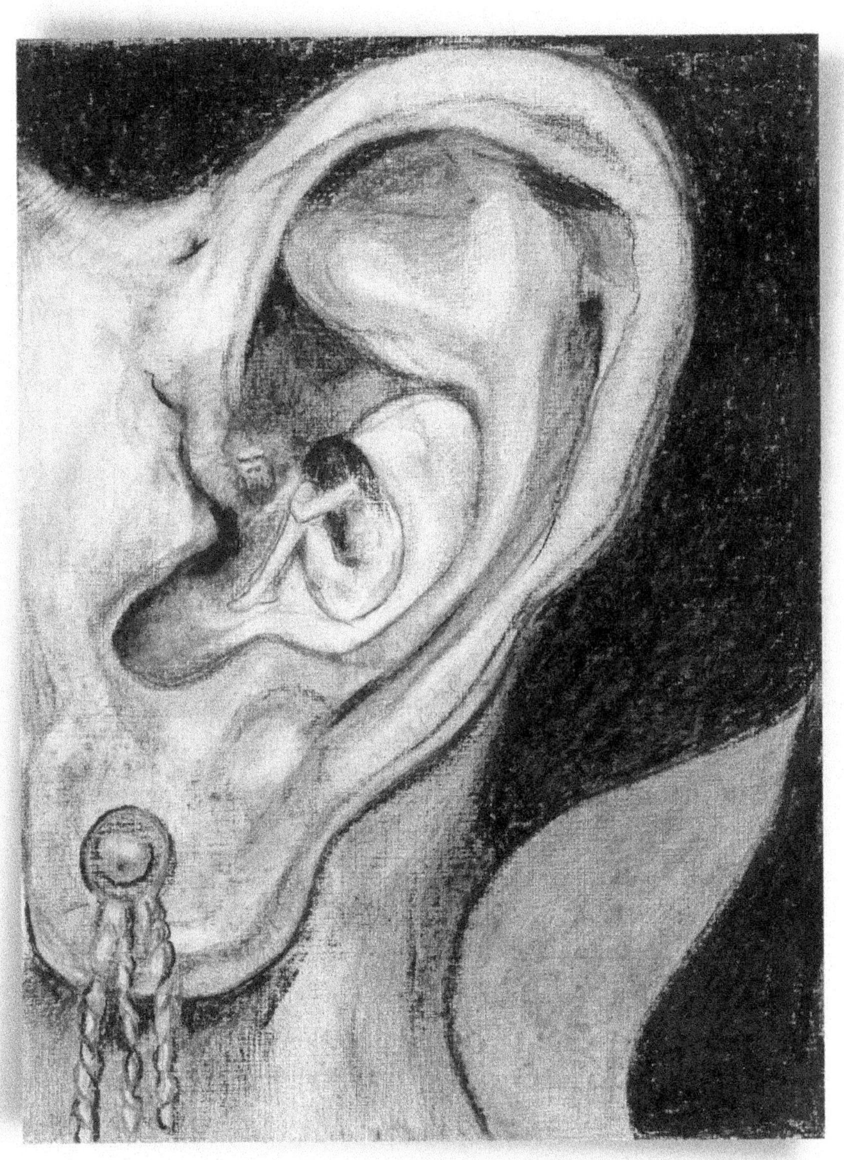

DAY 10

When I prepare dinner and my daughter doesn't eat, I take it very personally. In some ways, I believe that we mothers are the queens of food in the family. When something like an eating disorder sneaks onto the dinner table, it seems to deliberately defy the love that is meant to be expressed through food and its preparation. Over time I have learned that food is not love. Love is what inspires the action of giving. It entails the generosity, understanding and desire for welfare, freely given and without expectation.

When my daughter refuses to eat, I think her mental world requires something else. Perhaps a ready ear, a warm hug, or simply... silent companionship. I approach her affectionately, with clear reasoning and, without relenting, I wait by her side until her mind and body are ready to receive.

In some ways I find it difficult, I get frustrated when someone refuses to receive what I want to give. It awakens old wounds of rejection, images of unwanted boundaries, and forces me to reconcile within myself the idea of receiving what is inside me and what is in others. There seems to be a divergence in my assessment of the acts of giving and receiving. Unravelling my inner tangling regarding the very act of serving and being served, being the giver or receiver of something, and what I expect others to receive from me, opens my understanding to the complexities of the paths of our individual psyches and how we form meaning.

"I must endure the presence of two or three caterpillars if I wish to become acquainted with the butterflies".

The Little Prince (Antoine de Saint-Exupéry)

DAY 11

My daughter's best friend came to visit. She refused to greet her. Her friend was very insistent; she wanted to give her a Christmas present. I had to tell her to come back another time. Days went by and she reappeared at the door several times with the gift. A very small box. I don't know why, but I told her to give it to me rather coldly. They were laxative pills to "help" my daughter lose weight.

The task as a parent of a child with an eating disorder involves protecting them from the harm he or she may inflict on themselves, and this includes looking after their environment. This task is not always clear-cut; it is just as easy to fall prone to mistakes of overprotection, with serious consequences for their development, as it is to underprotect them when they need it most.

"When a man's neck's in danger, he doesn't stop to think too much about sentiment".

Agatha Christie

DAY 12

Over the months, some physical symptoms have appeared as a result of my daughter's malnutrition. Paleness, very low body temperature, reflux and abdominal distention problems, not only because of the amount of stomach acid but also because of the implication of other organs. Her skin is dry, she has insomnia, lethargy, amenorrhoea, purple lips and hands, hair loss, increased body hair, bad breath and many other symptoms... Each one is a warning sign from the body, which prompts me to continue to seek help for her speedy recovery.

I AM RECOVERING TOO

The premise that a mother can do something to stop the course and extent of her child's illness has long haunted my mind, albeit unconsciously. Today I rest assured that I do not have the power to stop any disease, but I can be at my daughter's side. Literature inspires me to be like a dolphin, swimming alongside her during the highs and lows of her illness.

"You've been so far away and I've been so close to you... I fear distance".

Alejandro Lanús

I AM RECOVERING TOO

DAY 13

I need some kind of help. What exactly it is, I don't know. I feel very lost, or maybe I'm losing my way. That is why I decided to go to the local church. I don't know what kind of church it is, it doesn't matter, I just understand that it is very close to home and I will be able to meet people from town. I liked that people are kind and I think the message of kindness is what I need. I will try to encourage my daughter, as there are groups of kids her age at this church.

As a foreigner living in a small rural town, there is a strong possibility of living a solitary life. I never thought I would feel so uprooted. But I do not believe that what I feel is good or bad. There are trees with deep roots and others that do not need to go so deep to grow. Now, however, I long for the closeness of my mother tongue and customs of my homeland. Today I wanted to ask my family if they could visit me. Such a surprise would make me very happy. I know it would do my daughter a lot of good to see her grandmother.

"It is wisdom to recognise necessity, when all other courses have been weighed".

The Lord of the Rings (J.R.R. Tolkien)

DAY 14

I am very worried about my daughter's low body temperature and I want to solve the problem. I put blankets on her bed and bring in the hot water bottle. I prepare her soup and steaming beverages. I turn on the heating, but she is still very cold. It is just one of several symptoms that I keep trying to resolve in my mind. She doesn't really want me to help raise her temperature. She throws off her blankets and puts on short-sleeved T-shirts. I find the hot water bottle on the floor. She turns off the heating in her room, flushes soup and food down the toilet or tosses it in the rubbish and sleeps with the windows open, all to burn more calories.

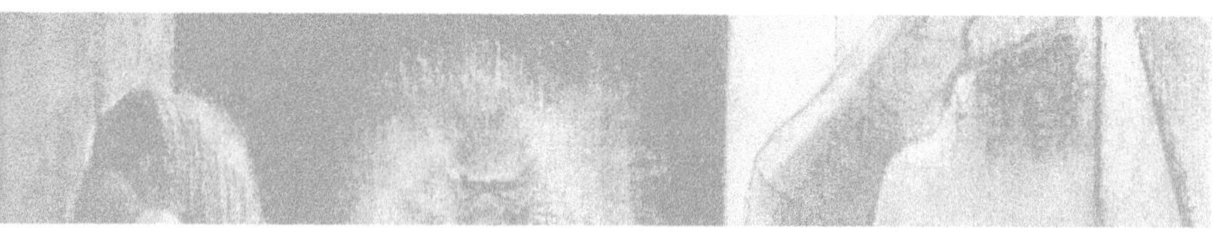

Insistence on seeking relief from the bodily symptoms of anorexia only makes sense if the reasons why it is important to receive care are explained to the boy or girl. I think I should have spent more time and energy talking to her before "helping" her with her body temperature on my own. Unfortunately, I was unaware at the time that there might be some limitation or shortcoming in her reasoning that could prevent her from seeking to align herself with her own recovery.

"Because experience, as a kind of knowledge, requires understanding".

Immanuel Kant

DAY 15

Come to think of it, my relationship with food has not been entirely good. When I am happy, I want to celebrate with food that I enjoy, but when I am sad, I don't feel like eating. In fact, yesterday I overindulged in chocolates. Same as the day before yesterday. And last week. I have also tried many diets in my life. If I look back at past generations in my family, I remember my mother doing a lot of dieting to lose weight and look slim. My grandmother hated cooking and kept telling us that. And looking back at my husband's ancestors, his family tends to overfeed. If I put it this way, I am not surprised that my daughter has gone from overeating to food restriction. I must be honest in my personal and family approaches to food.

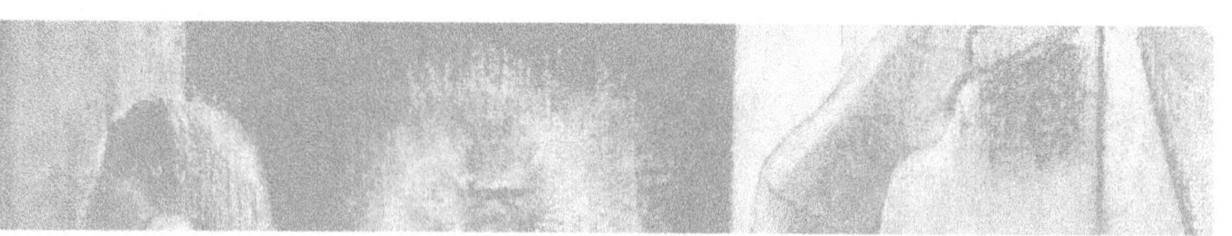

I started my psychological treatment with a therapist in the town where I live. It overwhelms me to think that I am going to spend an hour away from home knowing that my daughter is not well. However, I am starting to look haggard, because I have been unable to sleep. My daughter and I spend a lot of time at medical appointments; I live in fear of bad news. Her organs are not working properly. She is at a very critical level of malnutrition. I feel so lonely.

"Love is taking a few steps backward, maybe even more... to give way to the happiness of the person you love".

Winnie-the-Pooh (Alan Alexander Milne)

DAY 16

My alarm button has been triggered so many times that I'm afraid it's stuck in that state. Time passes and I see my daughter's paleness and thinness, her lack of energy, her teeth darkened from vomiting, her thinning hair, her purple hands. I wonder when things will start to get better. I notice that I live with the fantasy of how I would like things to be. I realise that I have not accepted reality, because I still think there is something better. That when she gets better, then I will be happy. The difficulty I have in accepting *what is* comes from what I think *should be*. A twelve-year-old girl should be 100 per cent healthy. Looking at it like this, it sounds a bit stiff. Even more so if I subject my idea of happiness to a rigid and static external conditioning. I don't really know from where, but that's how I live that fantasy.

Today I realise that happiness is unconditional. That with or without an eating disorder, there is room for happiness; because happiness is an idea created from my own mind. This is where I move meanings and it seems that if things are not the way I want them to be, then I will suffer. For a child, on the other hand, happiness is the present. I have decided to rediscover the happiness of a child, who appreciates life as it is. I choose to live happily today, regardless of the circumstances.

"I cannot for the life of me see why children have to take so long to grow up. I think they do it on purpose".

Matilda (Roald Dahl)

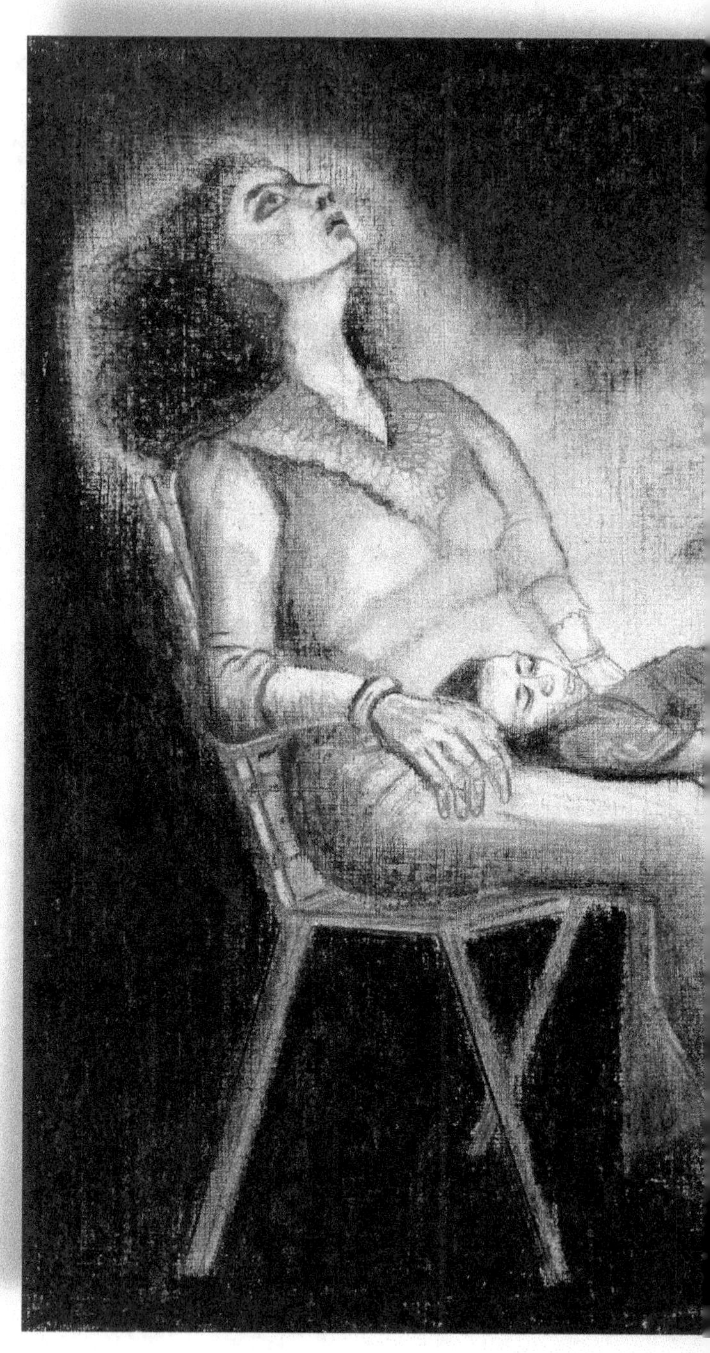

I AM RECOVERING TOO

DAY 17

A number of rituals have started to appear around my daughter's intakes. I watch her spreading the carbohydrates out all over the plate, separating the meat from the vegetables, and cutting the food into tiny morsels before putting it into her mouth. She uses dessert cutlery for the main course, drinks lots of water and goes to the bathroom several times to weigh herself on the scale. She ties her abdomen with a string, exercises in the evenings, drinks water with lemon to cut fat, wants to be a vegetarian and orders vegetables (leafy greens only) such as exotic lettuces. She chews gum all day. She spends all her time watching cooking shows on the internet or TV, looking for tips on how to lose weight. She wants to go for walks and runs after meals. She hides food so I can't prepare it. These are just some of the rituals.

I think I'm completely hooked on my daughter's rituals and behaviours. Wherever I go I find hidden food and it infuriates me. I can't help it, she's very unhealthy and I feel like I'm part of a game where she's always ahead of me in ruining her own health. Unfortunately, at the moment I cannot release her without putting her health at risk. My priority is managing my own emotions properly.

"Either I don't understand what is happening or what I understand has already happened".

Carlos Monsiváis

DAY 18

I have been angry with myself for not recognising that the dinner I prepared yesterday was going to trigger my daughter's anxiety. It was her favourite dish when she was little, but not anymore. How I miss the days when she smiled and looked so happy playing at being a mum! I feel sadness for what is no more, and I mourn that loss. She is also feeling anxious at the moment and dealing with it in her own way. If I drop the value judgement of every emotion and feeling, I will allow myself to feel; then, together, we can be.

Anxiety, sadness, anger, are vital parts of the self. If we avoid them without any qualms, we will be creating dead masks with frozen smiles that look outwards. But feeling lets us understand and know ourselves. It is from that feeling that we can ask for help, even if the feeling itself overwhelms us. Feeling is the present, I don't need to worry about foreseeing anything, because I live in the present with who I am. By doing so, I can also let others be and feel.

*"Weeds are flowers too,
once you get to know them".*

Winnie-the-Pooh (Alan Alexander Milne)

DAY 19

I remember every time I went to see the psychotherapist in England with my notebook. During our meetings (which were rather quick, as I was overwhelmed with thoughts of my daughter home alone), I wanted to know how to raise her. I wasn't interested in talking about myself, there was no time for that. I came eager for helpful advice to make sure my daughter could get better quickly. Specifically, I wanted things to return to "normal". I went there looking for solutions. I remember leaving those sessions frustrated and feeling very disappointed because the therapist always wanted to know more. She had asked me to put all my terror, frustration and desires into words.

The power of verbal discharge has brought about significant changes in my personal life. It wasn't always easy for me and, to be brutally honest, I only went to therapy for the first two years in the hope of helping my daughter. I did not always understand "the process" as I expected quick, impactful, painless and frustration-free solutions. But just as a body massage provides relief to contracted muscles after the session and can be painful during the procedure, talk therapy does the same. It can bring improvements after several sessions. Considering the way I am, talking therapy has been a great help.

"I feel more or less like someone who had their head in the clouds and then suddenly fell down".

Winnie-the-Pooh (Alan Alexander Milne)

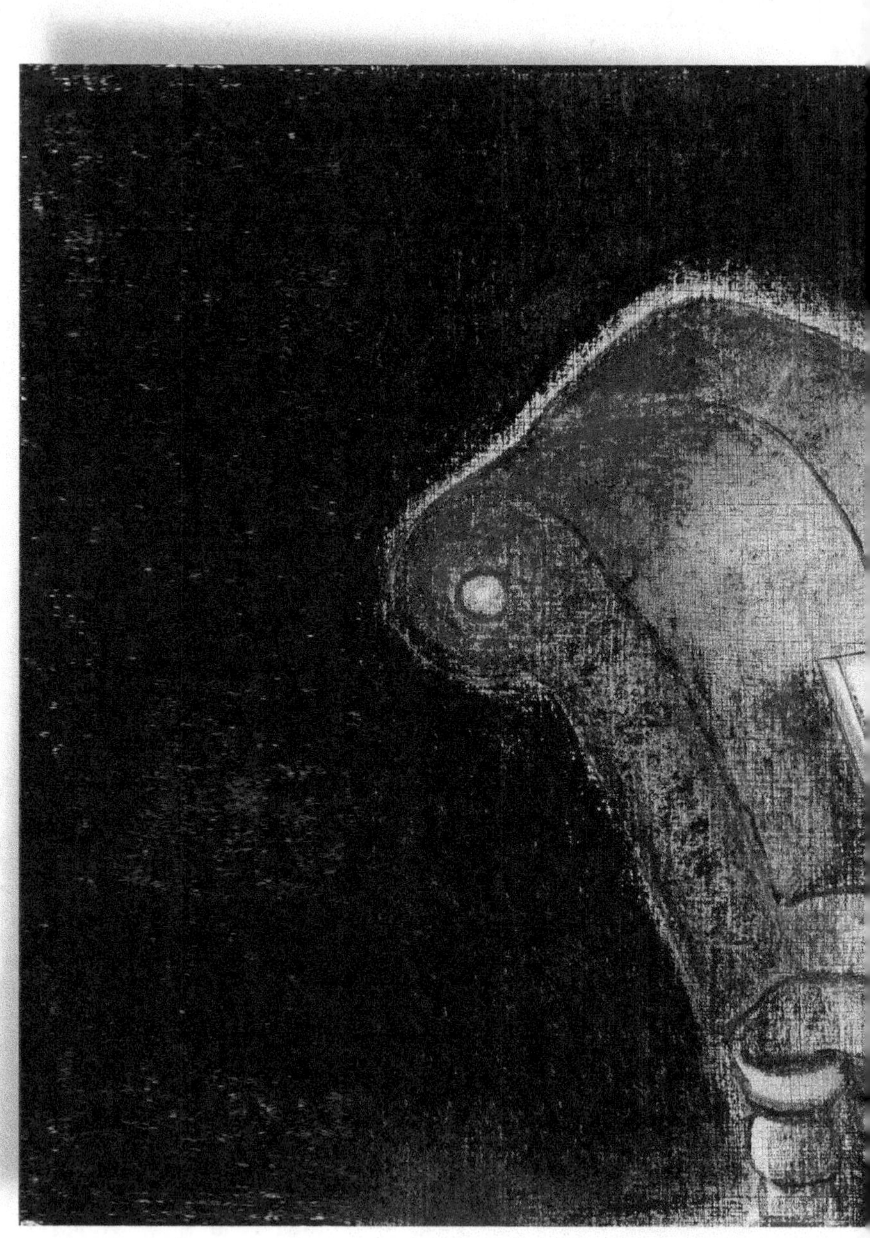

I AM RECOVERING TOO

DAY 20

It is sad to discover that mental health illnesses come with a stigma. I heard some ignorant comments in the church that symptoms of mental health illness are the result of demonic possession. Such comments only isolate entire families with or without mental health difficulties, depriving them of sharing and receiving the love and understanding they so desperately need. At the same time, there are warm people, full of affection and love, who make all worries vanish, accept us and offer us their company, cheerful and unconditional.

Caring for my daughter twenty-four hours a day, seven days a week, leads me to believe that there is no life without illness. That's why today I decided to go visit a friend. I need a change of pace. A friend is a refreshment to the soul when that friendship is sincere, warm and wishes the best for the other, without judgement or expectation. I hope with all my heart that my daughter will have good friends.

"After all, one can't complain.
I have my friends".

Winnie-the-Pooh (Alan Alexander Milne)

DAY 21

Last week I dreamt that someone close to me died and I mourned their departure. And last night I dreamt I was pregnant. The mind has extraordinary ways of revealing our inner selves to us. When I think about it, I do believe that something inside me died. My fanciful expectations of how things should be died. *What was not* died, to welcome *what is*. Often a death generates life; the seed falls to the fertile soil and must die in order to germinate, to grow, to bear fruit; the caterpillar's body falls and dies so that the butterfly can emerge. There is a transformation in this metamorphosis. There is room for something new. A new and living story that is woven day by day not on the basis of what should be but on what is new, fresh and unpredictable. I welcome the new that is coming, that is already germinating in me.

The wonderful world of dreams when we sleep, those stories where everything is possible, allow us to see how our mind works in the unconscious. There are hidden truths there, full of symbolism, which can reveal realities about who and how we are. This infinite register of mental movements, of adjustments and swaying, forms the unpredictable scenario where anything can happen. Free of judgement, unfettered; that's where we are, limitless and free.

"Don't you know that everybody's got a fairyland of their own?".

Mary Poppins (Pamela Lyndon Travers)

DAY 22

The reading material for parents of children with eating disorders tells me that I should not be a jellyfish, i.e. a mother who cries all the time. It also tells me not to be a rhinoceros, i.e. an angry mother who force-feeds or just reproaches. I should also refrain from being an ostrich, pretending that my daughter is not sick with an eating disorder. Rather, I should be a dolphin, accompanying her through the highs and lows of her illness.

When placing the existing reading materials and guidance under the lens of practical life, I believe that I am all animals at different times. I have even experienced them all at once in a span of ten minutes. I love my daughter but not the eating disorder, so sometimes I want to cry in anger and pretend that it is not my job to be the mother of a girl with this condition. In all honesty, I would add the bird to the theory of possibilities, because sometimes I would like to fly far away to where there is no such thing as eating disorders. I try to be the dolphin; however, the dolphin also has its challenges. As a dolphin mother, I have to accompany my daughter without suffocating her, take care of her and make sure she does not put her life at risk, but give her autonomy and a flexible agenda, as she is a teenager. There is some tension in how these difficulties can be navigated without doing further damage.

"Understanding means being able to do".

Goethe

I AM RECOVERING TOO

DAY 23

Today marks a great victory: my daughter has finally started eating those things she couldn't get down for the past few months. I understand that it is her victory and that she really needs much more than a full plate of food. However, it is a triumph to see her eating. She racked up quite a few days of getting only a minimal amount of food, which is alarming and extremely dangerous for her health. I wonder what worked. The anxiety component of this condition may be waning. She has been at home for several months without socialising except with her cousins. I am aware that the social aspect is somewhat difficult for her, as she was mistreated by her classmates at school. I am so openly overjoyed that I have been thinking about the session with the therapist about amalgamated or merged families. These are relationships in which it is difficult to differentiate oneself from the other. An amalgamation of me and my daughter is quite possible, as I have no family around me, my husband travels constantly for work, and we spend many hours together at home.

I have decided to arrange a transatlantic trip to see family in Los Angeles, California. This way my daughter can spend time with girls her own age, and I can spend time with my own. I have relied on my daughter's therapist in England to coordinate this trip. Although there are many variables surrounding this decision, I am certain that it is necessary to go out and change the environment. I am quietly uneasy about the possibility of deterioration, as my daughter will be exposed to different foods and new social environments. At the time, I saw this challenge as something huge and difficult to overcome, almost impossible, but we did it!

"It's funny how some distance makes everything seem small".

Frozen (Jennifer Lee)

DAY 24

My daughter has been eating a little more calmly for several weeks now. Eating in front of the TV is very helpful. We sit together and have dinner watching a programme that catches her attention. I feel the pressure to make sure she stays in school, as she is just starting secondary school. I am burdened with the responsibility of looking after her health, her social life and her academic programme. I have started to look for local homeschool groups. I really need support. The coming months will require all my energy to keep up with their studies, their nutritional plan and the natural vigilance that all mothers exercise around their children's interpersonal relationships.

My own recovery has gone down the drain. My husband dipped into depression which has taken a heavy toll on our family. Every day I do my best to continue to meet the needs of my daughter and husband. If I cover my basic body hygiene essentials, and schedule one phone call a week with a friend while we sort out the crisis, I'll make sure I don't slip into neglect.

"We are all connected in the great cycle of life".

The Lion King (Linda Woolverton, Irene Mecchi and Jonathan Roberts)

DAY 25

It has been several months since my husband recovered. However, my daughter does not feel very confident about returning to school. I definitely feel that she needs specialised therapy. For the time being, we'll stay at home. I have found a plan that structures the exams leading to her GCSEs or secondary school diploma in England. Her eating remains stable; however, there are days when I don't understand her reflux and paleness. I question my ability to help her. I do not feel that systematically forcing her to eat (as indicated by the guidelines of the local social security medical centre) is the right way for her. I have been unable to find a child therapist specialising in eating disorders. Her psychologist is not specialised for this and I don't really think continuing with her is the best option.

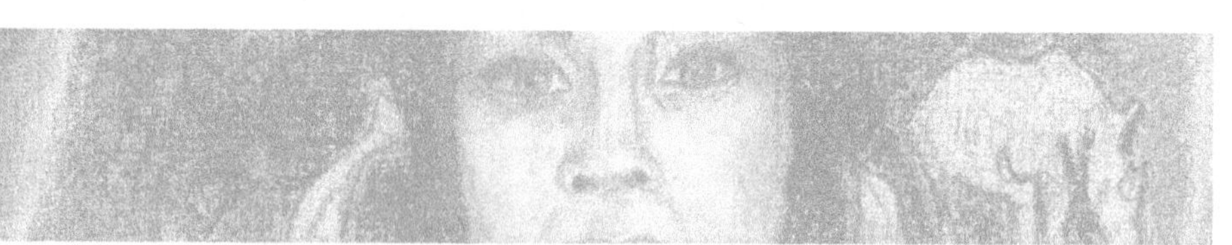

It is only now, after several years, that my daughter talks to me openly about her experience with the child psychologist. Lack of knowledge about eating disorders can lead to many mistakes. I feel it is necessary to stress that there is a big difference between being treated by the right person and settling for the wrong one. We had to wait three years before we could find someone qualified. The insistence warranted it. Appropriate therapy can prevent the disease from becoming chronic.

"The flower that blooms in adversity is the rarest and most beautiful of all".

Mulan (Rita Hsiao, Chris Sanders, Philip LaZebnik, Raymond Singer and Eugenia Boswick-Singer)

DAY 26

I have found someone who can help me with the cleaning at home once a month. In such uncertain times this person has become my family and my support. Having this kind and loving companion at home, even once a month, has allowed me to delegate certain tasks. She also alerted me to how chronic my daughter's vomiting was. I had not yet realised this and I am saddened by her suffering. I am aware that my daughter needs much more than what she is getting. She needs professional help. While I get it, I decide to move forward in my task of becoming a mother. The thought crosses my mind that a pet, a dog, would be a great birthday present for her and the whole family. Together with my husband, we decided to talk to our daughter and reiterated how much we love her, and that this love does not depend on what she chooses to do; it is unconditional.

Our dog Max has become a very important member of the family.

All the time I have spent alone and in silence over the last few years has been revealing and very productive in my inner life. Silence has allowed for introspection and has become a source of health and peace. By being alone, I have really learned to be with myself. Years ago I couldn't stand myself because I wasn't curious enough to know myself; in fact, I think I dreaded the idea. I was looking for affirmation outside, in others. I think I still have a lot to discover in my inner self. However, I am getting closer and closer and I know that I am on my way to fully enjoying my presence. In my opinion, self-knowledge solidifies an indestructible foundation.

"To laugh at yourself is to love yourself".

Mickey Mouse (Walt Disney and Ub Iwerks)

DAY 27

What if my daughter dies? Why do I whip myself with these meaningless questions? I know death is a possibility. Still, what is the point of tormenting myself with something over which I have no control? That question leads me to think that inside me there is an omnipotence, a grandeur that wants to control everything. In reality, death is a certainty for my daughter and for all of us, because we are all going to die one day. There is certainty in death. Yet life is uncertain. Rather, I must concern myself with life, with today, with my part in this daily life. Suddenly I rethink: What if I care about that living part of me and give it that bit of eagerness, commitment and attention it deserves every day?

Today I understand that taking care of myself also contributes to my daughter's wellbeing. Anything I can do to unburden my mind, attend to my body and develop my social, spiritual, professional, creative and recreational life contributes to my own health. I can only take care of someone else when I am well.

"To live... will be an awfully big adventure".

Peter Pan (James Matthew Barrie)

DAY 28

I have tried to keep the lines of communication open with my daughter. It is the most effective way to help her and to help me. However, it has not always been easy. The times when her condition has caused her to lie to me, find food in the rubbish, or see her vomit, I feel the difficulty of navigating the tone and content of conversations. Then we are completely alone. She finds socialising quite difficult and I find relapses very complex. Since she has been home-schooled, the decline in her social life and her noticeable deterioration have reinforced the amalgamation; socialising has become increasingly difficult for her. I have made it a point to invite several families from the church to dinner, and thus ensure that we have visitors on a regular basis.

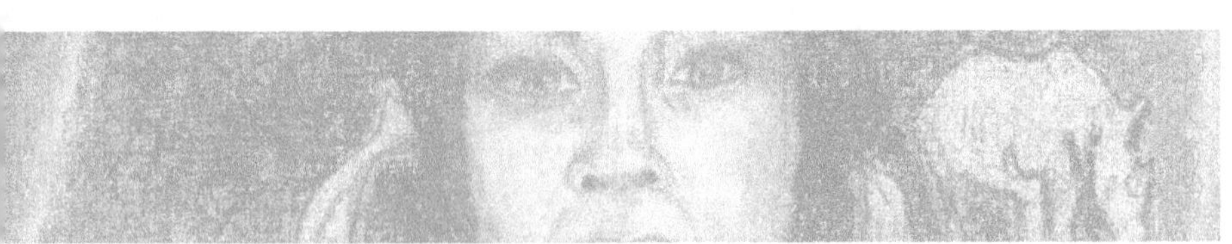

Family life with a loved one who has an eating disorder can revolve around the illness. I believe that opportunities to go out and interact with other families, as difficult as it may seem, are an important factor in recharging and stabilising the family environment.

"Coexistence is essentially knowing how to share and participating in the lives of others, while allowing them to become involved in our own".

Enrique Rojas

DAY 29

Today I woke up with an urge to run. I was never an expert runner. In fact, I hated running in school. Today, however, I would like to run and run without stopping. I want to run away. At 7:00 a.m. I went to my daughter's room. Seeing her so pale since the birth of the day, her appearance so gloomy, and breathing in that strange smell in her room, my thoughts return to the idea with which I opened my eyes. I look at her and, without reacting overtly, I want to have a normal conversation, but I am paralysed. There is a surging whirlpool swirling round inside me. I feel hot, I'm sweating. I look out through the window. I repeat to myself: today will be a different day, not one of those days when we fight this battle alone. I have no more strength to carry on. Intimately I have a feeling that the journey is going to be a difficult one. Deep down, I have begun to doubt that my daughter will be able to complete secondary school.

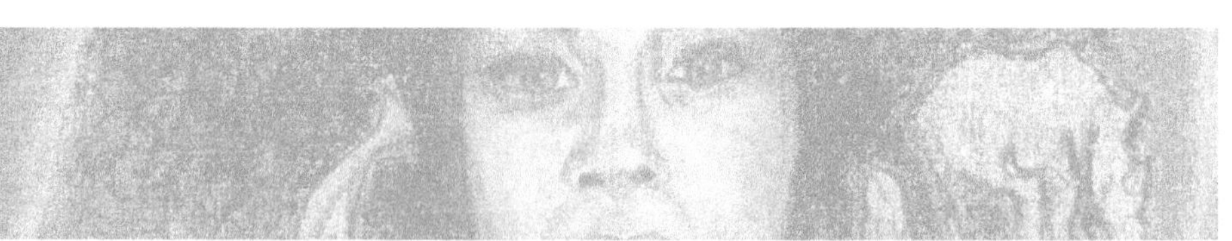

Everything in my thoughts is under my control. And this is the way I represent the moment I am facing. If I anticipate failure, a disappointment, then I am the creator of my own suffering.

In reality, every thought I have is a decision. And that thought has a value, a specific weight that influences my day in a powerful way. Only by discovering that I am responsible for my thoughts, I can live differently each and every situation I face. I will try to expand the possibilities for this time, including the ones I have already considered. Whether or not she finishes school is left to be seen. Nothing is set in stone. This gives me an idea of the true freedom that allows all possibilities to be given free rein.

"You are braver than you believe, stronger than you seem and smarter than you think".

Winnie-the-Pooh (Alan Alexander Milne)

DAY 30

The media, video clips, and social media saturate us with the idea of unhealthy skeletal bodies and miracle diets to achieve such forced thinness.

If I listen to conversations of ordinary people, the subject of dieting seems to be present at all times. It is quite possible that we are moving towards a cultural pattern that promotes total ignorance of our bodies and how they really work. I think we have found one more piece in the big jigsaw of what we know as eating disorders.

Every time I see "diet culture" in action, I ask myself how I can live unmoved by such public health nonsense. An important component is daily grocery shopping. I no longer buy diet products or low-calorie foods. I want to get back to healthy eating that covers all the food groups, including good oils and fats, and I know that in doing so I will be running against the tide. In fact, I will run for my own health and my whole family's health.

""I'm Short and fat and proud of that!!".

Winnie-the-Pooh (Alan Alexander Milne)

DAY 31

"And what is your relationship with your own body?" That question took me by surprise. My automatic response was: Well, no one has a "relationship" with their body. A relationship is only between two living beings, people or animals. After a while I thought about the mathematical relationship between the parts and the whole. And I resolved to clarify what was going on: that I live my body in my head and my head has no body. After reflecting on it further at home I realised that my relationship with my body includes my thoughts and attitudes towards it, my body image and satisfaction or dissatisfaction with the way it looks through my own lens. And seen from that perspective, my relationship with my body was never good. To begin with, I lived the body in a kind of state of denial; that is, the body didn't exist, and it didn't exist because I didn't like what was there. I always thought I had something to improve, something that wasn't right. My arms too fat, my back too wide, my stomach too big. The list was long. All this showed me a great lack of compassion and loving care for my own body.

There is an interconnected life system that makes it possible for my brain to send signals to my body. This connection is automatic and involuntary. In the same way my emotions have an interaction with the physical and corporeal part of my being. Today I am convinced that my thoughts, attitudes, feelings and beliefs can have a direct impact on my physical functioning. My relationship with my body has developed through self-care, knowledge and self-recognition of how my body functions at all levels. It is an important part of restoring my physical and mental health.

"The past can hurt. But the way I see it, you can either run from it, or learn from it".

The Lion King (Linda Woolverton, Irene Mecchi and Jonathan Roberts)

DAY 32

Although my daughter's body weight and intake are not at the lowest levels, today the doctor diagnosed her with chronic depression. I am convinced that my daughter needs a mental health doctor to help her. I am distressed to see her continue to suffer without professional support. I have discussed this with her and we have made the decision to start filling out forms for her to return to complete her secondary education certificate at a local school. She is eager, as she has a great interest in learning. Today, after three years at home, my daughter returns to school to take the final steps in her education. When thinking about how she has studied, her grades were a great achievement. I hope that the school will have a psychology department that will refer her to a therapist, and that she will be able to socialise with kids her age. Although uncertainty overwhelms me, I choose to think positively and hope for a recovery in the future.

Despite not having access to health professionals, my task up to this point has been to inform myself, read and learn more and more about eating disorders, nutrition, adolescence, mental health and homeschooling in order to understand how to help my daughter.

For reasons beyond our control, we had to move from home—this has made my life and my daughter's life less stable. Neither she nor I have access to psychotherapy anymore. I admit that these moves have been downright difficult for me. However, there is a small school where we are going, where she has been enrolled and will be able to get her certificate.

"I'm not crazy. My reality is just different than yours".

Alice's Adventures in Wonderland (Lewis Carroll)

DAY 33

Today I took my daughter to serve as a volunteer with rescued dogs. It is a job that caught her attention. I think it is important to look for areas of personal development that attract her and help her to have contact with other children; this also allows her mind to be elsewhere. I don't like it when she watches cooking shows on the internet or on TV, as they inevitably send false signals to her brain that her stomach is full. Now that I know more about eating disorders, I see the amount of junk messages on TV and the internet that can do a lot of damage to a person affected by eating disorders.

A peculiar feature of this generation is the proliferation of small families; with major consequences for the emotional and social development of the only child. As the mother of an only child, there are socialisation needs that are key to remember. In my experience, I believe that only children grow up differently because of their permanent contact with adults, mum and dad. Motherhood is also more intense, as all the family interaction of the only child falls on the mother. That was my case, and although I love my daughter and enjoy her company, I have always wanted to make sure she can socialise with kids her age.

"Children know such a lot now, they soon don't believe in fairies".

Peter Pan (James Matthew Barrie)

DAY 34

Finally, now that my daughter is almost 16, we have found a professional specialising in eating disorders. Several years have passed and I can only hope that there will be days of less suffering for my daughter. We now have psychiatric help, a clinical psychologist and a nutritionist. In addition, she has been assigned a general practitioner who takes a holistic approach to her health, threading together all treatment, both physical and mental. Entering secondary school has been a huge social challenge for my daughter. Her body weight and intakes have dropped considerably. I am concerned about her chronic malnutrition. Now that she is in school, I am relieved that I am no longer bearing the burden of her academic and social progress. However, her deteriorating body mass is a cause for concern; we have a considerable list of medical exams to carry out. I would very much like the company of a loved one.

My task as a mother is evolving. My active roles as a therapist, friend, teacher, psychologist, and nutritionist have all been addressed by trained health professionals. It is a relief to be able to resume my maternal role, which is still to accompany, provide an active presence and listen to my daughter whenever she needs it, support her with her treatment, and take her to her medical appointments whenever necessary. These transitions in my role as a mother require energy, and knowing how to tune in to the demands at hand as I go along. I want to get back to my own activities. I started with painting and I have also decided to start volunteering with an NGO that helps young people with drug addiction.

"Don't underestimate the value of doing nothing, of just going along, listening to all the things you can't hear, and not bothering".

Winnie-the-Pooh (Alan Alexander Milne)

DAY 35

We have received new guidelines, such as not talking about the body or food at home in order to help get rid of the obsessive part in my daughter's mind; another is to prepare normal dinners and lunches without fearing that my daughter will refuse to eat what is served on the table. I have also been taught what is the right portion of food for her. And even if she is anxious, it is precisely this anxiety that will be treated during her clinical therapy. I welcome the guidelines with gratitude, as it offers us a new platform, with the hope of its improvement. There is a belief that I treasure inside me, an expectation, a wish; now that my daughter has professional help she will get better quickly and without relapses. I believe that I am experiencing true recovery, that now she is going to stop suffering, and so will I.

Everything has its time, and its moment. A single medical professional, no matter how dedicated, cannot alone guarantee the improvement of any patient. In particular, mental health recovery requires time, energy, commitment from the patient and their family or loved ones, and above all, patience. Recovery has its ebbs, flows, advances and relapses; it includes better and worse times, suffering, silences, pauses, and of course, the longed-for victories. I have begun to work on the part called "family fusion". I have realised that I have been overfeeding myself for several years. This is explained by my desire for my daughter to imitate me. I have to start realizing my personal and individual needs are not the same as my daughter's needs.

"Rivers know this: there is no hurry. We shall get there some day".

Winnie-the-Pooh (Alan Alexander Milne)

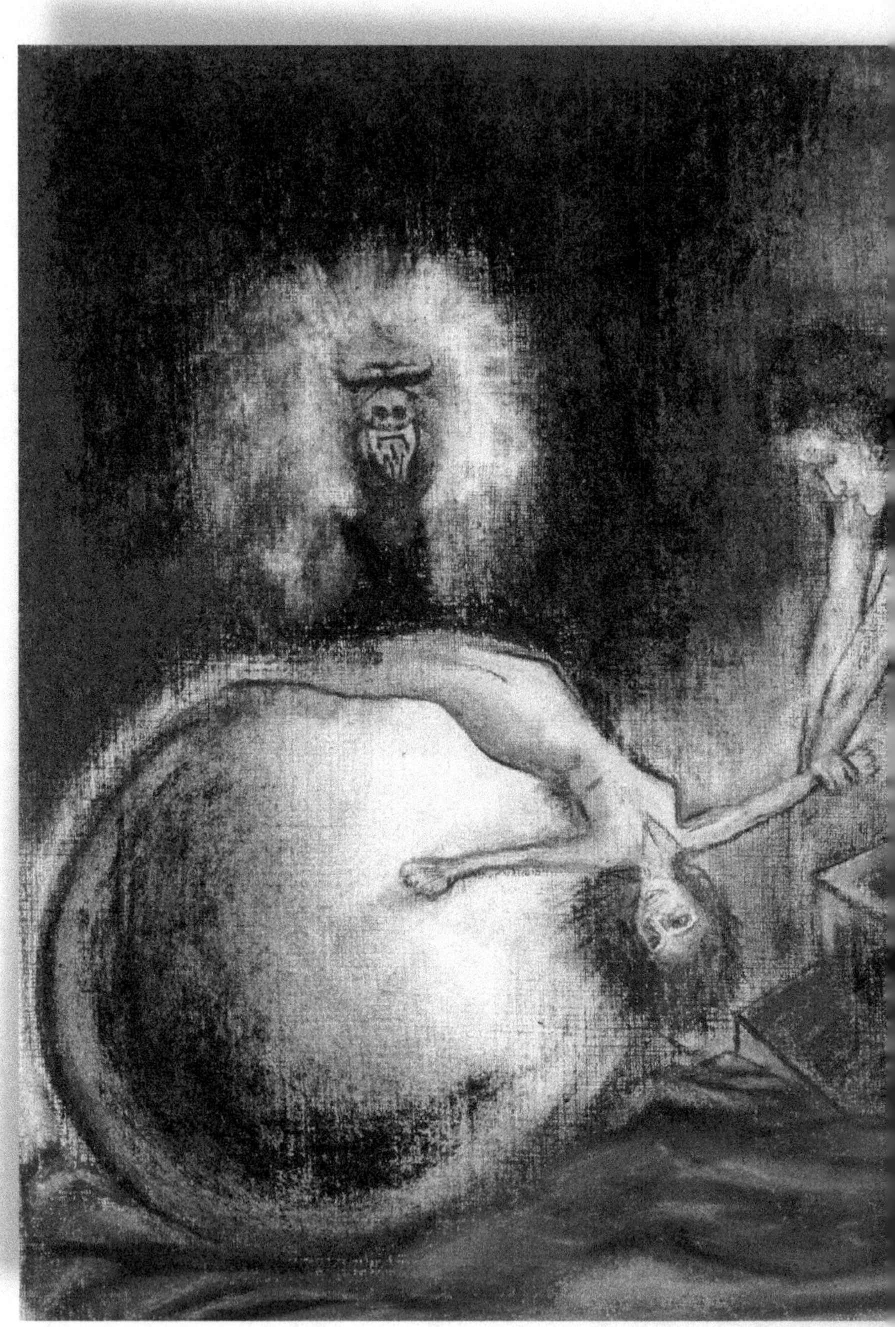

I AM RECOVERING TOO

DAY 36

My daughter's anxiety levels are sky high now that she has started school. Although she already has access to specialised psychological and psychiatric therapy, I have noticed that she is hurting herself, self harming. She cuts herself on her abdomen and sides. My daughter's suffering is evident, as is her difficulty in coping with social situations. All of her friends are struggling with conflicts and mental health challenges. Talking to her, I sense a great sense of guilt. I assure her repeatedly how much I love her. There is no reason to feel guilty. My husband now works from home, which is a great support for me and my daughter.

We all evolve and there are systems that have to go through long, cold and dark corridors to develop. It is part of the process. I think it happens to all of us. Feelings of guilt, anxiety and disillusionment can be swirling climates in families, affecting everyone at home. Yet these climates also change. My daughter's anxiety and guilt lead me to reflect on my own anxiety and guilt. Ultimately, I feel guilty, there is anxiety in my behaviour, and this has been the case since before the disorder started in her; but I also feel that my anxiety and guilt have evolved. I must begin to understand this fact about myself. I am going to start therapy again, as I feel it is necessary to help me.

"I knew who I was when I got up this morning, but I must have been changed several times since then".

Alice's Adventures in Wonderland (Lewis Carroll)

DAY 37

This morning my daughter collapsed at the dining table. The doctor at the hospital told us that she had suffered vasovagal syncope. It is a sudden and brief loss of consciousness. What struck me, however, was that as she came to, my daughter was temporarily unable to see out of one eye. She seems to have overtrained at the gym; she told me herself that she was trying to complete two hours of hard exercise and it was probably too much for her. The doctor suggests keeping her overnight for observation. My daughter doesn't want to stay and eat the food they serve there, because she's not familiar with it. A fragile mental space is tricky to navigate; more harm than good can be done. It is very important to ensure that she eats, otherwise her life is in danger. At home we have decided to take care of her and set limits on exercise. Her therapist and family doctors decided to run more medical tests to ensure her wellbeing.

I feel tired of worrying about what might happen. I know that there's no way I can prevent long-term health consequences for my daughter because her malnutrition is now not only critical but also chronic. Five years have passed and I understand that the pattern of recovery in a patient with an eating disorder is not linear, but upward spiralling and circular. The same challenges always arise, yet through an evolving process, which is backed up by learning from past experience. Even if the patient relapses, it is not a setback, as the knowledge acquired from the last time an event occurred is available. Reading helps me to sort out my emotions. I have ordered two more books.

"Some people care too much.
I think it's called love".

Winnie-the-Pooh (Alan Alexander Milne)

DAY 38

As time goes by, and as I look at how things have developed in our family, I suddenly see a path. I feel as if a path has opened up that I haven't seen before. Nothing has changed and everything has changed. It's because I now have a new lens within, and I see things differently. I love my daughter, and for the first time I don't see her as separate from her eating disorder. Today I see it as a whole. I think this is called acceptance.

I have wanted to define acceptance as an express or tacit act of receiving, assuming, welcoming, approving, embracing all the components present in another person, be they physical, mental, spiritual, rights, burdens, conditions, limitations, qualities or strengths, without qualms or wanting to change anything about them. Her eating disorder is a coping mechanism that her brain used in order to be able to function regardless of how much of a traumatic situation she was in.

"Grown-ups never understand anything by themselves, and it is tiresome for children to be always and forever explaining things to them".

The Little Prince (Antoine de Saint-Exupéry)

© Galia Carolina Smith MSc, PhD.

DAY 39

Back in England I hope there will be more progress on my daughter's recovery. Since we arrived (almost a year ago), my daughter has lost a lot of weight. As we follow the COVID restrictions, I am amazed at how frightened everyone is. I think I have been living quietly for a long time with a lot of fear of death. Perhaps because of this, COVID is somewhat similar to me and that is why I can handle it. You have to be considerate of others. I don't know their difficulties or how they fight their battles. At home, my daughter has just told me that she does not want to continue with her medical treatment, neither therapeutic nor psychiatric. In England, being almost of age, she is free to make her own decisions, ignoring her parents.

When faced with an unfamiliar problem I find it uncertain and challenged by the fact that I don't have an exact answer. I haven't known what is going to happen for quite some time. The one thing I have learned about uncertainty is that it must be dealt with calmly; and that it is best to concentrate on what is within my competence and control in the short term. Having clear goals and discerning what is really important to me brings me great clarity and peace.

"A little consideration, a little thought for others, makes all the difference".

Igor -character in Winnie-the-Pooh (Alan Alexander Milne)

DAY 40

Today we had a graduation ceremony for my daughter's IB program of secondary education. I feel relief and supreme gratitude, with God, with life, with my husband, with the therapists who have helped us. But most of all, I am so proud of my daughter! She is a warrior.

This achievement is hers, not mine, as it would have been easier for me if she had not studied and had done handicrafts at home. I welcome it because it shows many other sides of my daughter. She is not only a sick daughter. She is also a young woman with personal dreams and ambitions.

At the moment she is pale, haggard and sluggish, but she made it. Her weight is the lowest it has been in recent years. Nevertheless, she achieved outstanding grades in school, and I admire her so much! Despite all her battles, she always had her sights set on achieving her goal. I never dreamed I would get this far. I choose to think that the best is yet to come, and even though the ceremony is via Zoom, as we are in COVID lockdown, I am so happy to know that my daughter achieved her personal goal despite her health challenges! After six months without medical therapy she decided to resume treatment with her therapist.

My daughter has inspired me to persist in my dream of being and living, despite the circumstances. She continues her battle, but better armed, with professional help and the unconditional support of her parents. I have begun to realise that life is not about avoiding battles at all costs, or pretending we don't have them; it is about equipping ourselves with the best tools at hand to bet on the best outcome. My daughter is not a disease, she is a young adult with ideas, dreams big and small, with many abilities and talents.

"What makes the desert beautiful, is that somewhere it hides a well".

The Little Prince (Antoine de Saint-Exupéry)

Over seven years have passed since my daughter was diagnosed with an eating disorder. She continues in treatment and has chosen to study psychology at an English university. The battles continue and so does the gathering of new tools to give my daughter quality of life. Only now, the baton of her own recovery is hers. I have started to paint and draw—forever loving my daughter and with a heart that is always willing to listen.

"I will love my daughter to the end".

Magic Johnson

THE END

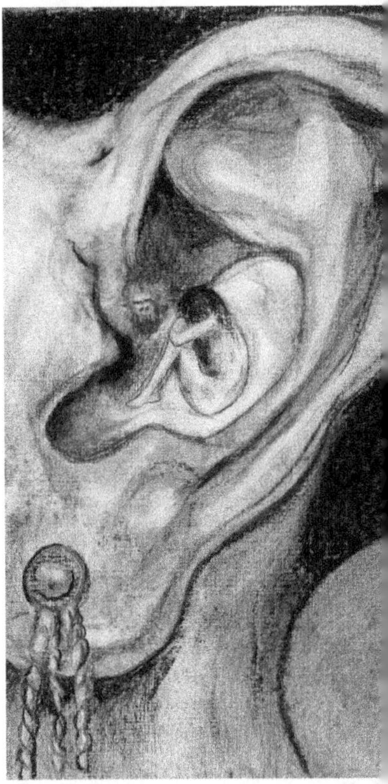

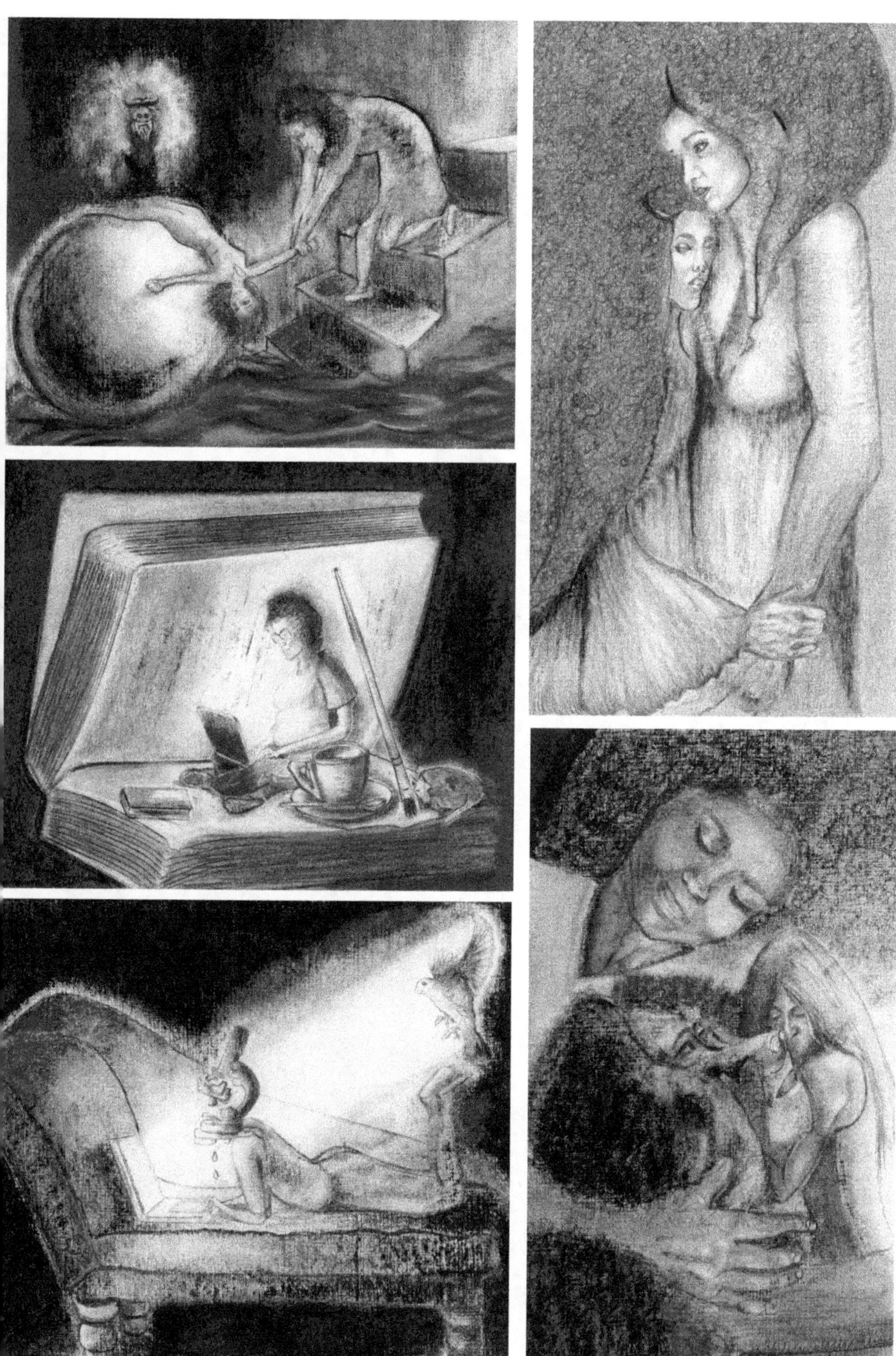

Author's Note: These illustrations are available as a therapeutic tool and visual stimuli for use within clinical contexts where parents and children receive treatment for eating disorders. iamrecoveringtoo.com